Splashes of Royalty

Greg M Cole

Published by Seven Frames Press, 2024.

While every precaution has been taken in the preparation of this book, the publisher assumes no responsibility for errors or omissions, or for damages resulting from the use of the information contained herein.

SPLASHES OF ROYALTY

First edition. October 31, 2024.

Copyright © 2024 Greg M Cole.

Written by Greg M Cole

Cover designed by Getcovers

For my incredible wife, Cheryl. Your love and encouragement continually remind me of Jesus. I am forever grateful that God has allowed you to be my life's mate.

Introduction

This book of poems and prayers is about relationship. The relationship that each follower of Jesus Christ has with our Heavenly Father. You see, we are the adopted children of God. The all-powerful, all-knowing, and all-present Creator of the Universe has adopted us into his family. God is our Father! This means that we can not only call him Abba (the Aramaic name often translated as daddy or papa) but also that we are royalty and heavenly heirs.

As followers of Jesus, we are also redeemed through Him. We did nothing to accomplish this. It was a gift from God that we did not deserve, but God gave it to us through his marvelous grace. This means we can come into the very presence of God – as his redeemed and adopted and royal children.

We can rejoice that we are redeemed and adopted, but we continue to struggle with exactly what it means to be royalty. We still "fall short of the glory of God" (Galatians 3:23 CSB). We are inconsistent in living our lives as royalty. Sometimes, we live exactly like the royal children of our glorious Heavenly Father. Other times, however, our thoughts, words, and actions are no different than those who have not been adopted and redeemed. We often live in *splashes of royalty*.

This book is my personal reflections of those **Splashes of Royalty** expressed through poems and prayers. Here is my attempt at sharing what our Heavenly Father is really like and what it means to be his royal child. As you step into my life through these poems and prayers, I pray that they will help you remember who you are – an adopted child of God and heir to an inheritance that will never perish (1 Peter 1:3-4). My hope is that these poems and prayers will move you toward living in the stream of royalty instead of just the splashes.

I encourage you not only to read these poems and prayers but to continue coming back to them again and again as they soak into your very soul, for they express the heart of what it truly means to be a royal child of God.

Living as a Royal Child of God

What does it really mean that we are adopted children of the King of all kings – the pinnacle of royalty? Preachers have preached sermons about it. Bible teachers have taught about it. Whole books have been written about it. But what does it mean to us when we personally and genuinely reflect on it?

It means, first of all, that God is our Father. He has chosen to adopt us into his royal family with full privileges of being the King's sons and daughters. Because we are royalty, we have an inheritance. The Apostle Peter describes it as "a priceless inheritance that is kept in heaven for you, pure and undefiled, beyond the reach of change and decay" (1 Peter 1:4 NLT).

Being adopted children of God also means that we have responsibilities. We are to live and act like the royal children we are. We are to live holy lives (set apart by God for God). When people see us, they should see our Father. We should think, feel, and act like him. What he loves, we are to love. What grieves him should grieve us. We are called to be "image bearers" of our Father Creator because we are made in his image. We are to live as the royal children we are!

Anything and Everything

Lord, you do not owe me anything,
But you have given me everything.
Blessing upon blessing,
Grace upon grace;
Poured out into my life,
Overflowing with your love.
Lord, you do not owe me anything,
But you have given me everything.
You are always faithful,
Even when I am not;
Your love abounds
Even when mine fades.
Lord, you do not owe me anything,
But you have given me everything.
When I fall short of your glory
Created within me,
You always forgive,
Setting me free from my guilt.
Lord, you do not owe me anything,
But you have given me everything.
You replace doubt with assurance,
Turmoil with peace,
Lostness with direction,
Despair with hope.
Lord, you do not owe me anything,
But I owe you everything.

Smile Into Eternity

I want to smile into eternity!
I want to enjoy
Each sunrise,
Each sunset,
Everything in between.
I want to breathe
Each breath,
In His favor.
Until the last.
I want to look back
At each moment
Lived as a gift.
I want to look forward
Seeking God's face
Listening for "well done!"
In this moment,
In this day,
In this life,
I want to live
In God's grace,
And smile into eternity!

Always

Lord, you are always!
Always present,
Even in dark places.
Always loving,
Even when I am unlovable.
Always merciful,
Even though I am undeserving.
Always truthful,
Even if it is painful.
Always faithful,
Even when I am not.
Let me sink into your presence today.
Let me embrace you
Forever into eternity;
As the everlasting, always God.

In Between

We live in two worlds,
Citizens of both;
Torn between now
And eternity.
Balancing both.

We live in the now,
A world of space and time.
We live the future,
A new heaven,
A new earth.
In between,
We wait...
For the coming of
Our Creator,
Our King,
Our Redeemer,
Our Father;
Abiding as royal children
With eternal inheritance.

Silence

Silence brings solitude,
But not quiet.
Alone with myself;
Thoughts reflecting
So mind-piercing loud;
Drowning the heartbeat
Of my chest,
Of the world,
Of the universe.
Silence shouldn't be deafening!
Silence shouldn't be difficult!
But it is!
Focus…
Feel the calm;
Feast on the quiet;
Let the waves of this silence
Wash over distraction.
Let reflection flow
From the past to now.
What in this day?
What in this moment?
What in this second?
Needs full-focused attention
For listening to the now?
As God speaks in the silence.

Except the One

In the down-stream of night,
Moon-tree shadows
Stretched barren arms
Along the broken sidewalks.
In our stolen dreams.
We waited for the dawn
To overcome the dark;
Sitting in the silence
Of our own breathing.
We listened to night sounds,
Scared, trembling together.
With nothing to grasp,
Except the One,
Who holds eternity
In his hand.

Fumbling Toward Faith

Somewhere between what is,
What could be,
What should be,
I lean into a wind called "future."
The trick is to lean hard,
Stay in balance;
Not too far forward
Or you fall through faith;
Not leaning back,
Or you fall into nothingness.
Where the Spirit leads me
Is a mystery,
An unknown known,
That unfolds in slow steps
Not yet taken,
But already walked;
As if...
Life is lived backward
From the mystery to the now

His Eternal Grip

His hand grasps mine
With eternal grip
To lead me out of darkness
Into light
His eyes pierce mine
With eternal grace
To show me I am loved
Unconditionally
His voice speaks to me
With eternal truth
To show what is right
And holy.

How is It?

How is it that we wait
For what we don't want
Eagerly, expectantly;
Eyeing tomorrow as if
It is some lost artifact
Aching to be found?
How is it that what we desire
Dies like morning mist
Tossed, tattered
Lying in the trash bin
Of brown-tinged boredom
And darkened disappointments?
How is it that we try
To be who we aren't
Bigger, better
Puffing ourselves up
Like helium balloons
Floating into nothingness?
How is it that we can't be
Who we really are
Authentic, absolute
Letting others see
Behind makeshift masks
Of indelible insecurities?
How is it that we fail
To let the Carpenter of Souls
Shape and sand
Us into something
Bright and fully beautiful
Looking like Him?

Immense Love

I praise you, O Great Three in One!
Father, who sent forth the Son.
Jesus who died on the tree.
Spirit who reveals truth.
I cannot comprehend your love for me.
I know it, yet I cannot fully know it.
I experience it, yet not completely.
I feel it, but only as a shadow.
Oh, Lover of My Soul,
Show me the depth, the breadth, the height
Of your immense love for me,
That I may praise you even more.

In the Beginning

In the beginning...
I wish I were there,
When light was born;
When God in majesty and mystery,
Spoke forth all we see;
Color waves blending into
A prism of white,
White into rainbow explosion.
In the beginning...
I wish I were there,
When the Triune Creator said, "Let there be..."
And there was!
Everything from nothing!
Always as planned;
Always as dreamed.
In the beginning...
I wish I were there,
For the first breath;
A living soul,
Created in his image,
Born to live,
Born to love,
As he loves,
In the beginning...
I wish I were there,
To behold,
To marvel,
The infant.
The light of the world;
Who became one of us,

That we might live in the light.
In the beginning...
Was the end;
New heaven,
New earth,
New beginning!

In The Midst

In the midst of knowing,
Yet not knowing
All I should know.
In the midst of being,
Yet not being
All I could be;
I wait!
I wait upon the
All-knowing One
Who is all-in-all.
I wait for,
His knowledge,
His wisdom,
His power,
To be.
Waiting is hard!
Depending is hard!
I think,
I desire,
To know,
To be,
What I want.
Because I am...
Yet, He is the only I AM!
He is the only all-knowing.
He is the only all-wise!
He is God
I am not.
So, I wait.

Life Is An Answer

Life is an answer...
To who I am,
To why I am here,
To what is important,
To whom I will serve,
To how will I live,
To how shall I die.
Life is an answer...
To questions
I never think about,
I'm always thinking about;
An answer I struggle with
Daily,
Hourly,
Every minute.
Life is an answer,
That can be right or wrong;
That I want to get right,
For my sake,
For other's sake,
For God's sake!

Lord, You Are Beyond All

Lord, you are beyond...
All understanding,
All comprehension,
All reality,
All reason;
Because they are all
Created and contained in you.
Father, this day I recognize
That you are
Incomprehensible,
Immeasurable,
Immutable.
You are beyond all.
Yet in your greatness
You choose to watch over
And care for me.

Morning Mist

Morning mist moves
Across a sleepy valley,
And silently sits
On beautiful blades
Of green grass,
Fresh flowers,
Towering trees.
Drops of life
Give rise to this new day;
Reflecting glory
Of the Creator;
Softly saying
To the whole world
I AM.

My Heart Breaks

My heart breaks,
For broken families;
Weeping for forgotten children.
My heart breaks,
For the ravages of war;
Weeping for justice to reign.
My heart breaks,
For humans who are sold;
Weeping for those enslaved
My heart breaks
Where there is despair;
Weeping for the hopeless.

I am prone to wander,
Where hurt overflows;
Weeping for those in pain.
I am prone to wander,
Where there is blindness;
Weeping for those who know Him not.
I am prone to wander,
From the God that I love;
Weeping for my wandering spirit.
Weeping for a broken world.
I am prone to wander!
Weeping for what He weeps for!

He knows how long, how deep, how far,
Are these wandering tears.
And saves them in his precious jar.

"You keep track of all my sorrows.
You have collected all my tears in your bottle.
You have recorded each one in your book." *

* Psalms 56:8 NLT

My Soul Settles

My soul settles
Into the safety
Of your presence.
My soul sinks
Into the steadfastness
Of your love.
My soul stands
In the security
Of your grace.
My soul rests
In the reality
Of your strength.
My soul longs
For more of you,
Everlasting,
All present,
Lover of my soul.

Never Changing

Morning moves into evening,
Night descends into dawn,
But God does not change.
My life is measured in years,
My body moves toward death,
But God does not change.
He is the same yesterday, today,
And tomorrow!
He is
Never ending,
Never changing,
Never failing.
God Almighty!

Newness

There is newness in this day.
That I will never know again.
Bursting into my life;
Welcoming what
I have not lived before.
There is newness in this moment;
Breathing deep to embrace
What I have yet to experience,
Surprised by each second.
There is newness in God;
Existing before time,
Knowing everything,
Experiencing everything.
Existing now, then, forever;
Yet always new!

Silence

Silence brings solitude,
But not quiet.
Alone with myself;
Thoughts reflecting
So mind-piercing loud;
Drowning the heartbeat
Of my chest,
Of the world,
Of the universe.
Silence shouldn't be deafening!
Silence shouldn't be difficult!
But it is!
Focus...
Feel the calm;
Feast on the quiet;
Let the waves of this silence
Wash over distraction.
Let reflection flow
From the past to now.
What in this day?
What in this moment?
What in this second?
Needs full-focused attention
For listening to the now?
As God speaks in the silence.

A Tunnel

There is a tunnel under life,
A tunnel deep and dark,
A tunnel deceitful and dangerous.
A tunnel that we fall into
Much too often.
Where thoughts spoil,
Where words kill,
Where actions hurt.
Where light is low.
Falling is easy!
A simple step
Into the Fallingness
Of long ago.
Living in my soul.
Escaping is easy too!
If pride is destroyed,
If selfishness is left behind,
If the Father is sought,
Forgiveness accepted,
His love embraced.

These Are the Words

These are the words of a rebel!
These are the words of a revolutionary!
These are the words of a radical!
These are the words that cut through
Logic and sensibility!
These are the words that counter status quo!

> *"Blessed are the poor in spirit,*
> *for the kingdom of heaven is theirs.*
> *Blessed are those who mourn,*
> *for they will be comforted.*
> *Blessed are the humble,*
> *for they will inherit the earth.*
> *Blessed are those who hunger*
> *and thirst for righteousness,*
> *for they will be filled.*
> *Blessed are the merciful*
> *for they will be shown mercy.*
> *Blessed are the pure in heart,*
> *for they will see God.*
> *Blessed are the peacemakers*
> *for they will be called sons of God.*
> *Blessed are those who are persecuted*
> *because of righteousness,*
> *for the kingdom of heaven is theirs."**

These are the words of Jesus,
God who became flesh,
Dwelt among us,
To show us how to truly live
As children of the King!

*Matthew 5:3-10 CSB

This New Day

This new day
Dances into existence
With two-step thunder;
Shaking sweet slumber.
I didn't ask for,
I didn't request,
I didn't want
This early wakeup call.
Covers pulled over my head
Pretending I'm asleep.
Didn't work with Mom either.

Another rumble ripples
Through this grey of morning.
And then, the rain starts
It's syncopated tune
Singing me into reflecting.
A decision needs to be made!
Do I get out of bed grumpy?
Or do I embrace this grey day
As a gift from the Creator?
I did not create this day of Grey upon grey.
With more undertones of more grey.
I would have made it
Sunshine and billowed clouds.
Brightness and stunning light!

The Creator saw differently,
He created it just as it is

As a grace gift.
A new day...
"To live,
To move,
And to exist in him."*
How I enter it is up to me.

Through the Waiting

Life is about waiting!
I can't wait until I'm old enough to...
I can't wait until I'm tall enough to...
I can't wait until the weekend,
my birthday,
Christmas.
Sometimes waiting is more than just desire.
It is a powerful passion of pain.
For those far away.
For those in harms way.
In hospitals, where everyone prays.
In hospice, counting life in days.
Wondering...
When?
Why?
What if?
How can we live through the waiting?
We live before the waiting...
In each moment,
In each word,
In each touch.
We live in the waiting...
In steadfast faith,
In total trust,
As we gain strength.
We live above the waiting,
Because he is Sovereign God,
That is in the waiting.

Where Do We Find Rest

Where do we find rest
In a world gone crazy,
Intensely insane?
It wears us down;
Wears us out;
Wears on our nerves;
Wears us down again.
When the latest news
Comes every mili-second.
Where do we find rest?
When stimuli is faster than thinking;
Processing becomes past tense,
Before it starts.
Where do we find rest
When rest eludes is at every turn?
We turn to the source;
The maker of rest.
He who didn't, doesn't, never will
Need to test!
But rested so that we can!

God Sees You

God sees you standing on the corner,
Listening for a life that is better,
A song that is sweeter,
A story that is safer.
God sees you standing on the corner,
Asking when the hurt ends,
Where the loneliness bends
Toward someone
Who will listen?
God sees you standing on the corner
Waiting for tomorrow;
Wishing you could forget today.
God sees you standing on the corner.
And so do I.

LISTEN!

Listen to the wind sing a song of far away;
Listen to the sun bring forth a new day.
LISTEN!
Hear your heart beat within your chest;
Hear your soul call out for rest.
LISTEN!
To each day as it lives,
To the wisdom that it gives.
LISTEN!
To the hurts that cry out in pain;
To the dreary days of drizzle rain.
LISTEN!
To your dreams wanting to live on,
Lost in the noise, then are gone.
LISTEN!
To your Creator speak,
Through every person that you meet.
LISTEN!

Today

Today is a day
That shapes me,
That lives in me;
That defines me;
That I must define.
How will I live this day?
That I didn't earn,
That I don't deserve,
That I can't expect.
With baggage of
Past mistakes
That I won't put down,
That I won't let go,
That I constantly carry?
How will I live this day?
With gratitude,
With simple joy,
Knowing it is a gift,
From Him who loves me
More than I love myself.

Praying as a Royal Child of God

One of the marvelous benefits of being a royal child of God is that we have the privilege of communing with our Father in prayer. In Matthew 6:9-13, Jesus teaches a model prayer - what we call "The Lord's Prayer." Almost every Christian has prayed this prayer, either corporately in worship services or individually.

> *In this manner, therefore, pray:*
> *Our Father in heaven,*
> *Hallowed be Your name.*
> *Your kingdom come.*
> *Your will be done*
> *On earth as it is in heaven.*
> *Give us this day our daily bread.*
> *And forgive us our debts,*
> *As we forgive our debtors.*
> *And do not lead us into temptation,*
> *But deliver us from the evil one.*
> *For Yours is the kingdom*
> *and the power and the glory forever.*
> *Amen.*
> (Matthew 6:9-13 NKJV)

It is a model prayer because Jesus told his disciples to pray this way when they prayed. I believe Jesus gave this prayer to us to pray aloud to the Father and as a pattern for praying. Each section can be used as a guide for our "Personal Lord's Prayer." The outline below is one way to use this model prayer as a guide to personalize your own Lord's Prayer.

Our Father in heaven,
Declare that you are a child of God and, therefore, you can call him Father. He is indeed your Abba; even though he is in heaven, he wants you to come close to him. James says, "Come close to God, and God will come close to you" (James 4:8 NLT). Tell him how much you love him.

Hallowed be your name.
Even though he is our father, God is still the sovereign, majestic Creator and Sustainer of the universe and is worthy of our praise and adoration. Spend time lifting him up and glorifying his holy - Name that is the Name above all names. Bow in his presence as your creator and savior.

Your Kingdom come on earth as it is in Heaven.
We live in a world that is blinded and battered by the forces of evil. God desires that our world be as it is in heaven. That happens when, one by one, people call on his name for salvation and healing and then submit to his rule in their individual lives. Pray that those who do not know the saving grace of Jesus will become an adopted child of God.

Your will be done on earth as it is in heaven,
God's Kingdom can only come on earth as his will is done on earth. This begins with each of his adopted children living as true royalty by obeying his will. Echo the prayer of Jesus in the Garden of Gethsemane – "...Yet I want your will to be done, not mine" (Matthew 26:39 NLT).

Give us this day our daily bread.
Peter tells us that God will provide everything we *need* in life. "*By his divine power, God has given us everything we need for living a godly life. We have received all of this by coming to know him, the one who called us to himself by means of his marvelous glory and excellence*" (2 Peter 1:3 NLT). Pray that your Father will provide for your...

- physical needs
- emotional needs
- social needs
- spiritual needs

Forgive us our trespasses, as we forgive those who trespass against us.
We fall short of who God created us to be – His royal children. We sin against God and against other people. Our relationship with others impacts our relationship with God. When we sin against God and against others, it grieves our Heavenly Father. Confess your sins and ask God to forgive you. He always will – "If we confess our sins, he is faithful and righteous to forgive us our sins and to cleanse us from all unrighteousness" (1 John 1:9 CSB).

Lead us not into temptation, but deliver us from evil.
This statement by Jesus is often misunderstood. God cannot lead us into temptation. James says, *"No one undergoing a trial should say, "I am being tempted by God," since God is not tempted by evil, and he himself doesn't tempt anyone"* (James 1:13 CSB). So, what is Jesus saying here? A better word for "temptation" would be "trials," for none of us is exempt from the trials of life. Pray that as you face trials in life, God empowers you not to let the trials cause you to sin, but to allow the trial to grow your character and your faith in Him.

For thine is the kingdom, and the power, and the glory, forever. Amen.
This closing doxology is not in the oldest texts, and most Bible translations do not include it. Yet, most of us end our recitation of the prayer with these words. There is nothing wrong with doing that. We just need to realize that Jesus probably did not say the words. If you want to include a closing doxology as you end our personalization of the Lord's prayer, you can say something like...

Lord, I proclaim that you have the power to bring about your forever kingdom! Help me to live as your Kingdom citizen right now, but always mindful of the future fulfillment of your forever, perfect Kingdom – a new heaven and earth.!

I want to encourage you to do two things to personalize the Lord's Prayer. First, develop your own personal Lord's Prayer in writing. Use it daily to follow Jesus' model. Second, use the Lord's Prayer as a guide for praying spontaneous prayers to him daily. May God richly bless you as you personalize the Lord's Prayer in your life! Here is my personalized Lord's Prayer.

Abba Father, who is in heaven
Let me this day...
Bring honor and praise to your glorious name,
For your name reflects who you are.
Let me live in your right now Kingdom,
Looking toward your Kingdom come.
Help me live out your will in my life,
As a model for others to follow.
Let me rejoice in your providing
Everything I need for life and godliness.
Reveal where I have fallen short,
That I might repent.
Help me to forgive others,
As you forgive me.
Give me power to say "no"
To everything not your will.
Protect me from the deceiver,
Who desires that I turn away from you.
Let your glory be reflected today,
In my every thought, word, and action.

*For yours is the Kingdom,
the power, and the glory
throughout eternity.
Amen!*

Emmanuel Greeting

Jesus, let this day resound with praises to You.
May my heart be filled with rejoicing,
May my words be filled with praises,
May my thoughts be focused on you:
For you are indeed Emmanuel,
God with me
Today, tomorrow, forever.
Let me experience the fullness
Of your presence this day.
Let me know that you
Are forever Emmanuel.
Hallelujah

Let Me Sink

Lord,
Let me sink into your presence,
Centering my life in you.
Let me sink into the reality
Of who you are ;
Deeply into the caring embrace,
That encircles,
Deeply into your astonishing grace,
That accepts,
Deep into your magnificent mercy,
That forgives,
Let me sink deeply into your love,
That transcends all that I was,
All that I am,
All that I will be,
Now and forever.

Help Me To Wait

Lord, help me to wait!
To not run ahead of You today.
Help me this day,
To live before the waiting...
In each moment,
In each word,
In each touch.
Because You are there before waiting. Help me this day,
To live through the waiting... In stedfast faith,
In total trust,
In your strength,
Because You are in the waiting.

Leaning Into This Day

Lord, let me lean into this day, By leaning into you,
Into your very presence,
Into your immense love,
Into your forever grace,
Into your total forgiveness,
Into your indescribable power,
Into your divine purpose.
Lord, let me lean into this day,
By leaning hard into you.

Let This Day

Jesus, let this day resound with praises to You.
May my heart be filled with rejoicing,
for you are indeed Emmanuel,
God-with me,
today and for ever.
Let me experience the fullness
Of your presence this day.
Let me
Hallelujah!

Living My Imago Dei

Oh, gracious and loving God,
Creator of my soul,
Who made me in your image.
As I live this day in your presence,
Recreate in me your likeness,
Of goodness,
Of truth,
Of beauty,
Of love.
That I may not disappoint you
By falling short of the glory
For which you created me;
That I may reflect you majesty
To all those I encounter today.
That I might bless you,
With every thought,
Every word,
Every action.

Passionately Seeking You
Lord, this day
Show me how to,
Passionately seek you,
Run hard after you,
Lean full into You,
Rely totally upon You,
That I might live today
As a sacrifice to you.
Help me today to...

Rejoice when You rejoice,
Grieve when You grieve,
Love as You love.
Help me this day to...
Live as You created me,
Made in Your image.

The Present Moment
My Lord and Christ,
Enable me to place complete trust in you,
To live in the present moment.
For you are ever present in every moment.
Help me not to run ahead of you,
but to savor each moment as a gift from you.
Help me to be still, to soak up your presence.
And with every breath,
Discover afresh the wonder,
The greatness of your love.

Goodnight, Emmanuel

Jesus, as I lay my head down tonight,
May my heart be filled with rejoicing,
For this day lived under your care.
May my mind be filled with reflection,
Of where I saw and felt your presence.
For you are indeed Emmanuel,
God with me
Today, tomorrow, forever.
You were present every minute of this day,
You will be present every minute of this night,
Even when I am not aware,
For you are forever, Emmanuel.
Hallelujah!

Rest, My Soul

Rest, my soul!
Rest in your creator.
Let Him bathe you in His care;
Let Him hold you in His silence;
Let Him wash away the dirt rings of yesterday.
Rest, my soul!
In silence;
In solitude;
Hiding the sounds of life,
As you hear only His breathe;
And the whisper of His love.

Focus My Senses

Lord, focus my senses toward you.
Let me hear your voice clearly,
Let me see you divine fingerprints,
Let me feel your loving presence,
Let me taste your mercy and grace,
Let me touch the hem of your royal robe
That I might be healed of falling short
Of the glory in which you created me.

Peace in Chaos

Lord, you promised a different kind of peace.
Please give me your peace today.
Peace that is above, beyond, an through...
Wars and rumors of wars;
Political turmoil;
Injustice, pain, and suffering.
Peace in the midst of my momentary
Troubles and fears.
Father, let me sink deep into your presence,
Knowing that you are always with me
Calming every storm - if I let you.
Give me this day,
The peace that surpasses all understanding.

Prayer For Contentment

Lord, move me toward being content in you alone.
Help me to focus my life in you
Instead of my longings.
I give you these stirrings inside me;
I give You my discontent,
I give You my restlessness,
I give You my wanderlust,
I give You my desire for something new,
I give You all the longings I hold inside.
Let them disappear into your presence.

A Prayer for Those Who Have Lost

Lord,
For those who have lost,
For those who mourn,
For those who lament,
For those with pain beyond bearing,
Bring comfort beyond comprehension.
Wrap them in the safety of your presence.
Wipe away their tears,
Lift their countenance of fear,
Turn their mourning into dancing.
Bring peace that passes understanding.
Let them rest in the comfort of your love.
Knowing that you are always there,
No matter what!

Morning Invitation

Good morning, Abba Father.
I invite you into my life this day.
Without any conditions.
Speak to me as you will.
Reveal to me where I have fallen short of your glory.
Show me how to live out your image within me.
Empower me to change where I need to change.
Empower me to live out your will this day.

Expectant Greeting

Lord, I greet this day
Expectant of
Your love
Your grace
Your guidance
Your discipline
Lord, I greet this day
With hope
With joy
With peace
With gratitude
Lord, I greet this ordinary day
You have created
For me to worship you.

Entrust to You This Day

Here I am, Abba, your Beloved.
By the Father - a humble servant,
By the Son - a follower of Jesus,
By the Spirit - a citizen of your kingdom.
I hereby entrust to you this day
My thoughts,
My word,
My actions,
To be lived in your power,
For your glory.
Amen.

Meeting This New Day

Lord, as I rise to meet this new day,
Let me be filled and empowered,
By your Spirit.
Wherever I go today
Let me spread love, joy, peace, and goodness.
Help me to think as you think;
Help me to see as you see,
Help me desire what you desire.
I thank you for always going before me,
Preparing the way.
I thank you for always being with me.
Showing the way.
May my life bring you glory this day.
Amen.

O Lord, Help Me This Day

Help me, O Lord, this day to reveal to you the ugliness in my soul,
for you already know it.
Help me turn to you with my feelings of anger and frustration,
for you always hear me.
Help me to rely upon your presence
and power to live the way you desire.
Thank you, Lord, for your patience with me.
Thank you for your faithfulness to me.
Never giving up.
Always present.
Even when I am not.
Amen.

Lord, thank you for this day,

That I did not bring into being.
Thank you for my life,
That I did nothing to create.
Thank you for my blessings,
That I did nothing to deserve.
Thank you for my salvation,
That I did nothing to earn.
May this day,
My life,
My blessings,
My salvation
Bring glory to you.

Teach Me to Live

Lord, teach me to live between two worlds.
Help me discover how to negotiate,
Being in this world, but not of it.
Help me to think and act today,
As your child,
Created in your image,
Heir to divine royalty.
Lord, help me to wait expectantly
For your return that ushers in
A new heaven and a new earth,
Where I will forever live.
In between, Lord,
Help me to live in this world,
Reflecting your glory,
Praising your name,
Sharing your love.

Resources

CSB - *The Christian Standard Bible*. Copyright © 2017 by Holman Bible Publishers. Used by permission. Christian Standard Bible®, and CSB® are federally registered trademarks of Holman Bible Publishers, all rights reserved.

NKJV - *New King James Version*®. Copyright © 1982 by Thomas Nelson. Used by permission. All rights reserved.

NLT - *Holy Bible, New Living Translation*, copyright © 1996, 2004, 2015 by Tyndale House Foundation. Used by permission of Tyndale House Publishers, Inc., Carol Stream, Illinois 60188. All rights reserved.

Don't miss out!

Visit the website below and you can sign up to receive emails whenever Greg M Cole publishes a new book. There's no charge and no obligation.

https://books2read.com/r/B-A-ACKOC-WCLDF

BOOKS 2 READ

Connecting independent readers to independent writers.

About the Author

Greg M Cole is an older guy with a young heart and attitude. He is passionate about communicating his thoughts and feelings through poetry. Why poetry? It has been said that poetry is good for the soul. It stretches the imagination. It brings the visual onto the written page. It communicates, in a few words, the interior of the soul. Greg has been writing poetry since his college days but now that he is semi-retired, he has the time to lean into his desire to write.

Greg is a Follower of Jesus and is passionate about sharing God's love through his writing. Therefore, many of his poems speak about the wonder, mystery, and majesty of a God who loves us beyond anything we can comprehend.

He lives in southern Colorado with his incredible wife, who is also his best friend. They have two wonderful sons, two loving daughters-in-law, and four grandchildren.

Read more at christformed.net.

Milton Keynes UK
Ingram Content Group UK Ltd.
UKHW030715051124
450766UK00001B/139